finding
Mr. Right

VONDIE LOZANO, PH.D.

ISBN-13: 978-0692827901 (Hearts Press)
ISBN-10: 0692827900

Hearts Press ♥ Ventura, CA

For my husband Henry,
my very own Mr. Right. ♡

And in loving memory of Paula Lozano...

acknowledgements

My first thanks go to Andrew Whaling and his Pasadena Sunday Night Singles group. Andy generously allowed me to share many of his dating tips in my blog and in this book. His step-by-step approach to dating also helped me find my wonderful husband.

Thank you to Terry Gorski for letting me share his "Blueprints for a Relationship" from his groundbreaking book, *Getting Love Right*. This framework provides the basis for my chapter on "Five Steps to Building a Healthy Relationship."

Special thanks to Casey Truffo, my brilliant marketing coach for many years, who encouraged me to start a blog which led to this book.

Many thanks to my awesome students, seminar participants, and clients. They were the inspiration for this book.

Grateful thanks to my family and friends for all their love and encouragement - especially my sister, Dia Anderson, and my friends Rani Bush, Nicky Fleming, and Kathe Caldwell.

A big thank you to those who helped bring this book to life: my talented editor, Elline Lipkin; my dedicated book designer, Susan Veach; my gifted photographer, Rico Mandel; plus Mishawn Nolan, Elaine OMalia, Lynne Klippel, Melissa Cassera, Evelyn Herrera, Don Stewart, Judy Cohen, and Debra Seabaugh.

And most of all, thank you to my husband, Henry, for his endless love, patience, and support, and for the beautiful life we share together.

table of contents

introduction
Stupid Things People Say When You're Single

When are you gonna get married?
Don't you know the clock is ticking?
Why are you still single?
You'll find love when you're not looking...

Sometimes people have good intentions. Sometimes they're insensitive. And sometimes they're just clueless.

When Are You Going to Get Married?

This comment is usually made by someone in your family who thinks you're great and can't understand why no one's snatched you up yet.

What they're implying is that you're being too picky — that surely, there are a ton of guys beating down your door and you're sending them all away. Or, they think you're too focused on your work, so you're certainly missing all the great guys going by.

Give them the benefit of the doubt. Maybe they don't realize you'd love to be married. Or that putting pressure on you doesn't help. It just makes you feel worse.

When this question comes up, just smile and let them know you haven't met the right guy yet. Then change the subject. If they come back to it, make an excuse to leave the room.

Don't You Know the Clock is Ticking?

Why would anyone ever say this to a woman? Are they trying to be funny? Or are they that insensitive?

Of course you know the clock is ticking. Sometimes it's ticking so loudly you feel like it's going to explode.

And you sure don't need someone else to point this out. If anyone mentions your biological clock, just walk away. If you can't physically get away, make it clear this topic is off limits and not open for public discussion.

Why is Someone Like You Still Single?

This one's kind of tricky. It sounds like a compliment. But, if a guy asks you this on a date, beware! It's basically a polite way of saying, *What's wrong with you?*

It's like he's sitting across from you thinking, *She looks cute... She looks normal... So, why's she still on the market?*

This sounds like he doesn't even want to get to know you. He just wants to find out why nobody else wanted you. OUCH.

Don't fall for this one. Don't even try to answer it. Just smile and say, "I guess I haven't found anybody who's right for me yet." Change the subject. And then move on... quickly. NEXT!

You'll Find Love When You're Not Looking

This is usually said by someone who met their husband or wife when they were really young and not even thinking about marriage.

Good for them. But what's their point?

Are you supposed to just sit there and do nothing and hope your future husband just happens to drop by?

I don't think so!

Again, thank them for sharing. And then change the subject. Then, find someone single to talk to who actually understands.

What Can You Do?

There is some truth in all of these suggestions.

You may have unknowingly overlooked some guys with potential. It is easy to get lost in your work if you really love it. You do have a time window to consider if you want to have a family. And there may be reasons you're still single that you might want to look at. And yes — you are more likely to meet someone when you're happy with yourself and just living your life.

But you are doing your best. And being pressured or put on the spot doesn't help. And being told to just keep waiting definitely doesn't help.

There are things you can do to meet a great guy. And there's nothing wrong with making that a priority. It means you want to get married and have a family. And why would you want to keep waiting when there's something you can actually do?

I.

Run Away from Mr. Wrong!

1.

How to Avoid "Hit and Run" Guys

Has a guy ever caused you to have whiplash? He comes on really fast. But then he runs away even faster.

In the beginning, he can't get enough of you. You're the most important thing in his world. But once you're really in the relationship, he backs off. He stops being so attentive. Eventually, he loses interest altogether. And it's just a matter of time before he walks out the door. And you're left wondering, "What just happened?"

You Got "In" the Relationship and He Got "Out"

You might have tried to put the brakes on at first. But he bowled you over with attention and affection. He was really persistent. And eventually, he won you over. You gave in. You decided to give the relationship a chance. But a funny thing happened. Just when you got "in" the relationship, he got "out."

The Faster He Comes On, The Faster He'll Go Away

The general rule is the faster they come on, the faster they'll go away. In the beginning of a relationship, it's all about infatuation and hormones. You may be a completely awesome person, but he doesn't know that yet. Because he doesn't really know *you* yet. So, he's not really falling in love with you. He's falling in love with a fantasy of you. That's why, as soon as the infatuation starts to wear off (usually around three to six months into the relationship), he'll start to lose interest. Because now you're becoming a real person. And, no matter how great you are, you'll never measure up to his fantasy.

He Likes Chasing You More Than Catching You

Men who come on really strong at first are usually more interested in the pursuit than the actual relationship. They like chasing you. They like wanting you. You're a challenge. But they don't actually want *you*. That's why they lose interest once you become interested. Somehow, you become less valuable in their eyes. That's why it's so easy for them to just walk away. They're eager to start chasing their next fantasy.

Some Men May Not Be Relationship Material

Granted, most men don't have that same nesting instinct that most women have. And many men also have some fear of intimacy buried within them. With these guys, however, it may be buried so deep, they're not even aware of it. As David Keirsey and Marilyn Bates discuss in *Please Understand Me: Character & Temperament Types*, some types prefer to keep their options open which can cause them to chafe against commitment. With "hit and run" guys, these things are all rolled into one package. All I know is the best way to deal with them is to avoid them in the first place.

How to Avoid the "Hit and Run" Guys

Andrew Whaling, Licensed Marriage and Family Therapist and singles expert, recommends several ways to slow yourself down and really get to know someone before falling in love. He says it helps screen out the "sharks" and "players" who aren't really interested in or capable of a real relationship. Whaling suggests:

- Date three people at a time.

- Space your dates two to three weeks apart.

- Don't get physical. (Whaling says a "goodnight" kiss is okay. But Louann Brizendine, a neuropsychiatrist and expert in female development, says women can get attached with a 20 second hug, so watch out!)

A Quality Guy Will Want You More

Only after the infatuation wears off will you know what a man is really like. Whaling says anyone can keep up an act for a time. Only after about six months will you know if he is actually who he appears to be and if he is a quality person or not. And a quality guy won't lose interest after he really gets to know you. He'll actually value you and love you more.

2.
Why Long Distance Relationships Don't Work

Long distance relationships seem so romantic. But the truth is, being apart for extended periods of time rarely works for long. According to Brizendine, couples need regular physical contact to stay connected. And this is especially true for men.

You Don't Really Get to Know Him

Plus, Whaling points out that when you're dating long distance you never really get to know each other. When dates are few and far between, you want to make the most of your time together. So everyone is always on their best behavior. This is a problem, especially in the beginning stages of a relationship, because he's not getting to know the real you. And you're not seeing the real him.

Date Within One Hour's Drive

The general rule is to date men within an hour's drive of where you live (or however far you are willing to drive to see him). You need to be close enough to see each other regularly and spend time at both your places and with your friends. That's how you start merging your worlds.

It's tempting to date men further out, especially if you're dating online. But remember, if he's outside your date-driving-range, you can't really get to know him. So, unless you plan to relocate while you date, don't go there, literally.

3.

Don't Let Texting Ruin A New Relationship

Texting is a great way to stay in touch. But, too much texting in new relationships can backfire.

It Goes Something Like This ...

He starts texting you after the first date. You feel kind of weird, since you just met. So, you try to discourage him by sending short texts back or by ignoring some of his texts.

But he doesn't get the hint. You'd like to give him a chance, but all the intense attention is sort of overwhelming and a little stalker-ish.

Or, maybe you really like him so it's fun to get all his texts. He texts you after your first date to tell you how much he enjoyed it. He texts you in the morning to say "hi." And he texts you at night before bed. You're sort of in a relationship, even though you haven't made it official.

But then all of a sudden the texting stops. You're not really sure what happened. But you were "talking" so much that it feels almost like a breakup.

Texting Lets the Fantasy Get Ahead of Reality

If you're texting throughout the day or even once a day it can feel like you're in a relationship before you really are. And, if he's really into you, he's going to assume all kinds of things about your "relationship" that you may not be ready for.

If you really like him and you're texting back and forth it can be fun at first. But all that instant, constant contact makes it way too easy to share too much too soon.

Sometimes one person isn't ready for all that closeness. Or there can be misunderstandings because you don't really know each other that well yet. Plus, you can misread things because you don't see body language or catch other signals that would be clear if you were talking in person or even on the phone.

Don't Let Texting Tank Your New Relationship

Set your boundaries right away when he starts texting you. You can let him know you like him by acting excited to hear from him when he calls or in a brief text telling him how much fun you had when you went out together. But, you can also let him know that you don't like to do a lot of texting. Tell him you need to take it slow.

A good guy will respect that and actually value you more.

When is Texting a Good Idea?

It's great to be able to send a quick text saying, "I'm on my way" or to send him directions. And one or two short texts between dates can be nice. Just remember, don't get carried away and say too much too soon.

It's easy to get ahead of yourself with too much texting. And that can sabotage your new relationship before it even has a chance to get started.

4.

Why Didn't He Call?

You think everything's great. You're looking forward to seeing him again. And then he says, those famous last words, "I'll call you."

You wait and you wait. You feel worse and worse. You sit by the phone. And you keep asking yourself — *Why doesn't he call?*

No Call After a First Date

Since he doesn't really know you yet, this is the easiest one to shake off. Sure, you're disappointed. And it would be better if he hadn't said he'd call or if he could let you know he's just not interested. According to Greg Behrendt, co-author of *He's Just Not That Into You*, a guy would rather lose a limb than let you know he's just not interested.

You've Had a Few Dates and He Forgets to Call

In the beginning, there can be mix-ups and misunderstandings. You're still getting to know each other and getting your rhythm down. If you don't hear from him when you expect to, there's always the chance that he actually forgot. This doesn't have to mean that it's over. That will depend on how he handles the mix-up.

When you ask him about the missed call, does he sincerely apologize? Or does he get defensive or come up with a big long story? If he takes responsibility without making you feel bad, that's a really good sign. On the other hand, if he blames you or seems to be less than forthcoming, that's a big red flag. And remember, in the beginning, this is him on his best behavior.

You're a Couple and He's MIA (Missing in Action)

If you're actually in a relationship, it hurts even more if he starts to distance himself from you. You may have a well-established pattern of checking in with each other. You talk every day. Or maybe you text throughout the day. And then something starts to shift. The texting slows down. He's not calling as often or he's not picking up your calls. You tell yourself it's no big deal, but something inside you says it is.

After the initial infatuation subsides, it's normal to have less intense contact. But, there's usually more regular contact and time together. On the other hand, if it feels like he's starting to back away, pay attention. And talk about what's happening. Otherwise, there's a good chance that the closer you get, the more he'll back off.

He's Gone Without a Trace

This one is the absolute worst. One minute you're in a relationship. The next minute, he's gone. He stops calling. He stops texting. He stops coming around. It's over. And you have no idea what happened. The most important thing to remember with this guy is that you probably didn't really know him at all. And it's really not you, it's him. But, you'll feel more empowered if you can see any red flags you may have missed.

Did he come on really strong at first? Remember, the faster he comes on, the faster he'll go away. Were there times that you ignored your instincts? The more you trust yourself, the safer you'll feel about trusting the next guy. Was he someone you could really see yourself with? Or were you settling for less than you deserve? Your guy will call because he'll realize how awesome you are. So that guy who didn't call — he's definitely not *your* guy.

5.

Rules for a Breakup: Can You Stay Friends with Your Ex?

Have you ever wondered what the rules are for a breakup? And what if you or he wants to stay friends? Does that really work?

Should You Stay Friends?

If he initiated the breakup, it's really hard to stay friends. Because deep down, you still really want to be with him. If you initiated the breakup, it's not fair to expect him to be able to just be friends because he's probably still in love with you.

Why "Friendly" Works Better than "Friends"

There's nothing wrong with being friendly if you run into each other. But it's usually best to keep your contact to a minimum. Otherwise, it's just asking too much of the person who still wants the relationship to work out.

Don't Sabotage Your New Love

It feels weird to cut someone out of your life after you've shared so much together. But it's hard to move forward when you've got your ex hanging around. Besides, it's not fair to your new love. You have built-in intimacy with someone from the past. And how can someone new compete with that? They can't.

As the Relationship Goes, So Goes the Breakup

If it was a bad relationship or bad breakup, it can be hard to be polite, let alone friendly. But if the relationship was pretty healthy overall, the breakup is usually more manageable. And that makes it easier to stay friendly.

Are There Any "Rules" for Breaking Up?

Do it Face to Face

It's pretty awful to hear that it's over via a text, email, or call. Of course, if you can't do it face to face, a call or text is better than nothing.

Use "I" Statements

"I don't want to go out anymore." (Not: "You're not what I'm looking for." OUCH.)

Don't Explain Why

When breaking up, *less is definitely more*. It never helps to give someone a list of all the reasons you don't want to be with them. First of all, that can be hurtful. And second, it gives them hope that if they can change those things they might still have a chance.

Make a Clean Break

Don't try to wean yourself off gradually. It never works. And don't keep tabs on him via Facebook, Twitter, etc. Any contact (even virtual contact) keeps you releasing bonding hormones that make it harder to move on. Plus, there's always the risk of getting re-involved. And definitely no breakup sex!

Give yourself plenty of time and space to grieve and heal (even if you were the one that initiated the breakup). This will help you get ready to get back out there again.

II.
Getting into the Dating Game

6.

Best Places to Meet Men

A while back someone suggested women take golf or scuba classes to meet men. So many women did this that there were more women than men in some of these classes!

Hanging out where the men are isn't a bad idea. But, the goal isn't to meet *any man*. The goal is to meet your man — *the man who's right for you.*

Here are a few of my favorite places where you might meet your Mr. Right:

Singles Groups or Clubs

The best singles groups are focused on something important to you — your faith, your politics, your love of the outdoors. This could be a church singles group, the Sierra Club, or any singles group with a religious or political focus. Then, when you meet someone you like, you'll already have important things in common. The group also needs to include people around your age who are looking for a real relationship. And Whaling recommends singles groups that have a steady stream of new people coming into them.

The Dog Park

If you're a dog lover, taking your dog to the park is a great way to get outdoors and meet new people (read: men). This is especially true at the dog park because you'll be meeting men who share your love of dogs. Plus, your dogs give you a built-in ice breaker. If you're a dog lover, but right now you're between dogs, invite a friend and her dog to join you.

Relationship Workshops or Seminars

Workshops or seminars where singles come together to learn about relationships can be a great place to meet men. These men are motivated to learn about themselves.

Friends' Get-Togethers

One of the best places to meet men is when your friends have people over. There's a good chance you'll have things in common with your friends' friends. Plus, your friends can give you the scoop on what he's really like. Just say yes when your friends invite you over for dinner or a barbecue or to play Apples to Apples. And remind them to include some single guys they like and respect.

Online Dating Sites

Everyone is using online dating sites. But, not all online dating sites are created equal. It's better if the site costs something and if it requires a lengthy questionnaire. The investment of time and money helps screen out men who aren't looking for a serious relationship. Some sites even prescreen your matches for you. This is ideal because it allows you to consider men who aren't your type. Remember, if your type hasn't worked for you in the past, it might be time to try something new.

Classes

Do you have a passion that you care about deeply? If you take a class in this area, you can meet men who also share your passion. The focus of the class might be the environment or horseback riding or dancing. What matters is that it's important to you.

I Met My Husband Swing Dancing

My husband and I met through the Pasadena Ballroom Dance Association (PBDA). They have a low-key venue that feels kind of like being at a wedding. People of all different ages attend. They offer dance classes during the week and free lessons at their Saturday dances — both are great ways to get to know people. A close friend also met her partner there. Thank you PBDA!

7.

Blind Dating: Why a Fix-Up Could Be Exactly What You Need

Just the thought of a blind date might make you squirm. But, if you think about it, most of your online dates are blind dates. Except you haven't had someone vet them for you. And that's the best part about blind dating. Someone else is prescreening your dates for you. That's why a blind date could actually be a great way to meet someone new.

Let Someone Else Pick for You

One of the benefits of a blind date is that someone else is doing the picking. If you tend to attract the same type of guy over and over and it never works out, it can help to have someone else pick for you. This overrides your basic chemistry, which means you might meet someone you would overlook otherwise.

That doesn't mean you won't have passion; it just may take some time to develop. And you might have a better chance at a good relationship with someone you're not initially attracted to. According to Thomas Lewis, Fari Amini, and Richard Lannon (experts on the psychobiology of love and authors of *A General Theory of Love)*, chemistry just means he's a perfect fit for all the hardwiring in your brain from your family-of-origin relationships.

All Matchmakers are Not Created Equal

All blind dates are not created equal because all matchmakers are not the same. You want to be set up by someone who really knows you and who has a good relationship of their own. Because, if they know you (and love you!) and have a relationship you admire... well, that's the kind of person you want to enlist! (If they don't have a good relationship, you might not want them choosing a potential mate for you.)

"I'd Love to Be Set Up"

I know, it's embarrassing to ask people to set you up. But it's not as hard as it sounds. The next time you're at a get together or party and someone asks if you're seeing anyone, let them know that you're not, but that you'd love to be set up. I know it's hard to say. But most people (especially women) love to play matchmaker. They'll immediately start thinking of their friend, cousin, coworker, etc. that could be right for you. And if you don't feel comfortable asking your guy friends for help, Whaling suggests asking their girlfriends or wives.

Try Something New

It's always nerve-wracking meeting someone for the first time. And you may have some bad blind dates. And there may be the occasional awesome blind date. But most of your blind dates will probably be somewhere in between. And that's okay. That's how you learn

to date and consider men you wouldn't normally choose. And if the people you've chosen
in the past haven't worked out so well, it might
not be a bad idea to try something new.

8.

How to Avoid Dead-End Relationships

Don't Waste Your Time

The last thing you want to do is spend a lot of time in a relationship that's going nowhere.

You spend a few months getting to know someone. You fall in love. You're together for a year or two. Things don't work out. You break up. And then you spend another year recovering before you're ready to date again. You've just lost a couple years (or more!) of your life and now you're back to the beginning. Whaling calls this serial monogamy. You're dating one person at a time, over and over.

Date Lots of Different People

Whaling says it's a "numbers game." Instead of wasting a lot of time on one guy, you want to date a lot of different men. And you want to go slow enough that you don't get attached before you really know them. That way if it doesn't work out, you just stop dating that person. That's it. No horrible breakup. No down time recovering. And you get to keep dating the other men you were seeing while you were seeing him. This translates into no time off the dating market.

Don't Put All Your Eggs in One Basket

Remember, Whaling recommends dating three people at a time and spreading your dates with each person two to three weeks apart. Because if you're going out with the same man every week, you're in a relationship. This also helps you go slow and not get too physical. And it keeps you from getting overly focused on one guy. Since it takes three to six months for infatuation to wear off, before then it's mostly hormones at work. That's why it doesn't make sense to become exclusive with one guy right away.

Smile and Make Eye Contact

How does Whaling suggest you find three people to date? You have to let men know you're open to being approached. Remember to smile and make eye contact even if you can only look at a new guy for a nanosecond. That's how you let him know it's safe to approach you.

Become a Dating Machine

You'll be amazed how many men you'll meet once you start smiling and making eye contact. The other thing Whaling recommends is to change your dating criteria. The only requirements for a first date are 1) You wouldn't be embarrassed to be seen with him in public and 2) He's age-appropriate (not old enough to be your father or your son). That's it. You can find out the rest once you start going out with him.

Do You Want to Get to Know Him Better?

The best part about dating more is you'll get lots of practice. So when you do meet someone interesting, you'll feel more comfortable. You'll know what to do and say. You'll be able to just be yourself. And you'll know how to take it slow. Then, you get to decide when you're ready to take it to the next level.

9.

Why You Have to Flirt!

Flirting can feel dumb, silly, coy. But according to Whaling, you have to flirt to attract the kind of man you really want.

Flirting Weeds Out the "Sharks" and "Players"

Whaling also explains that a good guy won't approach a woman without some sort of signal that she's interested because he doesn't want to get shot down. So, when you see someone you think is interesting, it's really important to smile at him and make eye contact (even if just for a second). It lets him know you're open to being approached. Whaling says if you don't learn how to let a guy know you're interested, you'll only attract the ones who are oblivious to what you want (not a good sign). Or worse, you'll attract the ones who are only interested because you're *not* interested ("sharks" and "players"). And those guys will usually lose interest once you become interested.

Flirting Says You're Ready to Take It to the Next Level

When a guy approaches you (at the bookstore, dance, etc.) pay attention to the signals you're sending. Are you smiling and looking at him? Are you answering his questions and asking him questions about himself? Do you feel comfortable facing him or moving closer while you're chatting? These kinds of cues let him know you're comfortable and are enjoying talking to him. Then it becomes completely natural for him to ask if you'd like to get together sometime.

Oops — He Misread Your Signals

Since flirting is mostly nonverbal, there will be times when you get your signals crossed.

When you do, it's not necessarily the end of the world. But it's important to take a step back. You can ask yourself what your actions and words are saying. Maybe you were trying to be nice, but you ended up giving the wrong impression. If you know each other a bit, it's okay to talk about what happened, so you're not just guessing. But if you're just getting to know each other, it might be awkward to bring it up.

You Need to Keep Flirting!

And you don't just flirt when you first meet. You need to keep flirting! That's how you communicate you like him and you're ready to take it to the next level. Some examples:

- Lean in to hear him over the music.

- Tap him lightly when he makes you laugh.

- Look into his eyes when he drops you off (meaning "It's okay to kiss me").

And once you're together, you still flirt! It's how you let him know you love him, you still think he's sexy, and you're so glad he's yours!

III.
Online Dating

10.

Shopping for Men!

What's not to love about online dating? It's basically shopping for men!

- You can shop from the privacy of your own home.

- There are lots of men to choose from.

- You can check boxes to order up men who meet your criteria.

- You can get to know men online before you meet them in person.

It sounds so easy. So, why do some women find love online and some don't?

#1 Online Dating Mistake

Have you ever gone shopping for lipstick and when you get home it turns out you bought the same color you already have? That's what happens with online dating. You can end up choosing the same type of guy over and over without meaning to. You might even make a conscious effort to choose someone different. But somehow, you find yourself back in the same type of relationship that hasn't worked in the past.

That's because chemistry works even on the Internet. But, all chemistry means is that he's a perfect match for the hardwiring in your brain that formed through your childhood and family relationships. The only problem is — if you don't want a repeat of the past — he may not be a perfect match for you.

#1 Online Dating Tip

Have you ever been shopping for clothes and the salesgirl brings you something you would never have picked out for yourself? But you try it on and it turns out to be perfect! That's what can happen with a great guy who isn't necessarily your type at first. He can turn out to be exactly what you're looking for.

There are 10% of men out there you're dying to kiss — run away from them! That just means they fit all the hardwiring in your brain from your family-of-origin. And if chemistry hasn't worked for you in the past, there's a good chance it won't work for you in the future.

Then there are the 10% who make you feel as if you'd die if you had to kiss them. You don't have to go out with guys you find unappealing. They might be exactly what another woman is looking for. But they're not for you.

But, the 80% in the middle — that's where you want to date. This just means being willing to take a chance on a new kind of guy — a good guy. And by good, I don't mean boring. A good guy might be cute, smart, and friendly. You might have a lot in common. He might be someone you'd have as a friend. There might not be a lot of chemistry at first. But it can develop.

You don't just want infatuation — you want love. And when you find it, you'll have the whole package — friendship, romance, and love.

Who could ask for anything more?

11.

Choose the Right Online Dating Site

Before you can find the right guy, you have to find the right site. Otherwise, you could find yourself looking for love on a hook-up site without knowing it.

Watch Out for Sexy Pics

Don't spend too much time checking out other women's pictures because you'll start comparing and criticizing yourself.

But you do want to make sure all the other women on the site aren't putting up super sexy pictures or worse — pictures where they're not wearing much at all. Because that means you're on a hook-up site.

If you'd rather not check out the women's pics, just look at the men's. If the guys all look like players (super-hot and sexy), you're probably in the wrong place. What these pictures tell you is that most of these guys aren't looking for love, they're just looking for sex.

Is He Willing to Spend a Little Money?

If you choose a site that's a bit of a financial investment it helps screen out the guys who are just throwing up a quick profile looking for something casual (again: read sex). It also means he's willing to spend a little to pay for the membership. That doesn't tell you a lot about his finances. But, if a guy isn't willing to spend anything he might not be ready for love.

Is He Willing to Work for It?

You also want a site that requires him to work a little. Some dating sites require a lengthy questionnaire. That up-front investment of time can also screen out guys who aren't serious about finding love.

Some sites even prescreen your matches for you. They use their research to choose men who would be a good fit for you. And then you get to choose from that pool. This overrides your tendency to keep picking the same type of guy who never works out. And when you find someone from this site's matches for you, you have the foundation for a pretty good relationship.

Do You Have Shared Values?

I've also seen people get married who met on values-based sites. These are primarily religious sites like JDate or Catholic Singles. The people I've known who met on these sites weren't particularly religious or active in their faith. They just wanted someone who shared their values and had been raised in the same kind of family.

Of course, you could get lucky on a free site with lots of sexy pics. But the goal is to do everything you can to stack the odds in your favor.

12.

Create an Online Dating Profile to Attract Your Guy

You don't want a ton of replies to your online dating profile. You want a few good ones because you are unique and special. And you want a guy who wants someone exactly like you!

The Right Pics

Men are visual, so your main picture is the most important part of your profile. Choose pictures where you feel pretty and happy because that will come across in the picture.

Besides the usual head shot, guys usually want to see the rest of you, too. Add some pictures that give him a small glimpse into your world — you on vacation, you walking your dog, you at a holiday party.

Other Pic Tips

- No sexy pics. You'll attract guys who just want sex.

- No pics with other people if you can help it.

- Not too many pics. You don't want to come across as a narcissist.

- And of course, make sure your pics are clear and recent. You don't want to feel you're doing any false advertising.

A Catchy Headline

What are your hobbies and passions?

- Are you a gourmet cook?

- Do you love to salsa dance?

- Do you love your grad program or career?

How do your friends describe you?

- Cute and endearing?

- Playful and silly?

- Serious and intense?

Combine some of your passions and personality into a catchy headline. You might be a Salsa Dancing Psychology Student or a Gourmet Cook Who Loves Dogs or a Sassy CFO.

Use your profile to paint a picture of who you are that makes him want to know more. And nothing sexy in your headline or the rest of your profile. (Just like a sexy pic — it will attract guys who just want sex.)

A Description that's Uniquely YOU!

You want to share what makes you different or special so that you get the attention of your guy. But you also want to present yourself in the best possible light. It's just like when you're looking for a job — you highlight your strengths and downplay your weaknesses. You put your best foot forward.

- Are you spontaneous? Say so.

- Are you whip-smart? Include that.

- Do you have a wicked sense of humor? Add that too.

If you're worried about sounding like you're bragging, say something like, *My friends say I have a wicked sense of humor.*

Another way to describe yourself is to share a story that reveals who you are. You might say, *I love to travel and try new things.* Then share a story that demonstrates this. *I went to Hawaii last summer with friends and I learned how to snorkel! My favorite moment was getting up close to a sea turtle. It was awesome!* You've not only shown him that you love to travel and try new things, you've also let him know that you have good friends, that you appreciate wildlife, and that you can swim!

But what if you're an introvert? And after a day filled with people, you can't wait to curl up with a good book or watch your favorite TV show? If that's who you are, share it. Just liven it up a bit. You might say, *I love getting together with my friends. But I also love a quiet night with a good book or watching Downton Abbey.* Opposites tend to attract. Your guy probably loves his friends, too. But, he would also love a quiet night curling up with you!

Your Deal Breakers

This is a tricky one. Let's say you're a vegetarian. Obviously, that's important to you. But you don't have to lead with that because there may be guys out there who haven't really thought that much about what they eat. But, they might be supportive and respectful once they understand what it means to you.

On the other hand, if you're a vegan for spiritual reasons and you could never be with someone who isn't a vegan, that's a different story. Go ahead and include this in a more prominent way. Yet, it's also important to keep an open mind. Your guy may not fit into the exact box that you're imagining.

Your Boundaries

Don't overshare. Even if you're an intense person, dial it back in your profile. Sharing too much too soon is a red flag. Think of it like a first date and keep things light and positive.

Be safe. Don't include identifying information through which someone could figure out where you live or even where you work.

A Little Help from Your Friends

Have a good friend look at your profile to make sure it sounds like you — at your best. If possible, have a guy friend read it. He can tell you how it will likely come across to your guy. And ultimately, that's what really matters.

13.

How to Spot His Red Flags

If you want to find your guy, you have to screen out the wrong guys. You need to read between the lines and trust your gut so you can spot the red flags!

He's Not Quite Ready for Love

Does he mention his ex anywhere in his profile? If he's still talking about her, he's not ready for YOU. Red flag.

Is he all the way divorced? No matter how he tries to spin it, separated is not divorced. Repeat after me: "Separated is NOT divorced." Red flag.

He's Got Issues

Does he sound angry or impatient? He may have "issues" from his past relationships that will back up on you. Everyone has issues. But, if he's putting his in his profile, that's probably a red flag.

Is he talking about sex? All men are interested in sex. But again, if he thinks it's a good idea to talk about it in his profile, that's kind of a red flag.

He Needs to Work on His Boundaries

Is he sharing too much? Do you feel uncomfortable reading his profile? He may have bad social skills. Or he may have a tendency to overshare and want instant closeness. If these are areas he's working on, these could be yellow flags. If these are blind spots for him, that's a red flag.

Is he sharing too little? He may have low self-esteem or be very private. These may just be yellow flags. Or it could mean he's not very invested in the process. That's a red flag. *Or worse, it could mean he's hiding something. That's a HUGE RED FLAG.*

If you decide to proceed, proceed with caution.

His Pics Are Inappropriate

Does he have a ton of pics? He may be kind of into himself.

Does he have a drink in his hand? He may drink too much.

Does he have someone cut out of his pics? He may not be very tech savvy. Or he's kind of clueless. These may just be yellow flags.

Does he have any pics where he doesn't have enough clothes on? Definitely not a good sign!

Is someone or something with him in all his pics? If so, then his car, his boat, his friends, or his kids will most likely come before you. You get to decide if this is a yellow flag or a red flag.

No pics at all? He may have really low self-esteem which could be a red flag. *Or he may not be who he says he is. Again, this is a HUGE RED FLAG. If you decide to proceed, proceed with caution.*

He Violates Your Deal-Breakers

You're anti-gun and anti-war. He's a gun-loving, pro-military member of the NRA. Stick to your guns! Seriously, if you start negotiating your non-negotiables, that's a red flag.

A Note About Yellow and Red Flags

According to Whaling three yellow flags equals one red flag.

So, how do you know when it's a yellow flag or a red flag? Trust your gut. And if you need backup, ask your close friends — the ones who have your back. They won't be swayed by his hot pic or charming profile because they want what's best for you.

And that's what you want in a guy — a good friend who has your back and wants what's best for you. Plus, you get all the romance and other stuff too.

14.

Be Smart and Guard Your Heart

Online dating makes it way too easy to create a fantasy in your mind of who this person is. The only problem is — it isn't real.

It's also way too easy for someone to pretend to be who they're not. That's why you have to protect your heart and be smart.

Don't Fall in Love with a Fantasy

Real closeness takes time. And no matter how much it feels like you're clicking with someone, you're still basically strangers in the beginning.

That's why you don't want too much contact before you meet. Whaling recommends no more than three to six emails sent via the dating site.

Have a quick call to set up the first date with no long conversations and no texting. Otherwise, all that sharing creates an illusion of who he is. And when you finally meet in person, it can be a rude awakening.

That's one reason long-distance relationships aren't a good idea. The fantasy can get way ahead of the reality. Plus, someone who's intentionally misleading you can use long distance to keep up the charade.

What if He Misrepresents Himself?

Maybe his profile says he's six feet tall. But it turns out he's a little shorter. Men lie about their height like women lie about their weight. These "driver's license" lies are usually forgivable. On the other hand, if it says he's single and he's married, that's an actual lie. And there's no excuse for that.

You can always Google him to see if he is who he says he is. There's even a way to Google his picture. Yes, it takes the romance out of things. But once you know him better, you can tell him about it. That way, it won't feel like a big secret.

Is He Too Good To Be True?

If you feel like he "gets" you better than anyone ever has, it may be because he knows just what to say to make you feel that way. Remember, real relationships take time. And con men and scammers do exist. So, keep your eyes and ears open. And trust your gut if anything feels weird or off.

If he says things that don't add up or make you uncomfortable, pay attention. For example, if he wants to keep emailing and is avoiding meeting in person, that's not a good sign. And of course, if he asks you to send him money, that's the biggest red flag. He may have excuses and long explanations for everything. But the general rule is — the more elaborate the story, the less likely that it's true.

For more information on scammers, visit the Federal Trade Commission website and click on "Scam Alerts."

Be Smart and Stay Safe

You probably already protect your personal information — your last name, your email, your address, where you work, etc. You may even use a Google Voice phone number or Vumber so you don't have to give out your real phone number. It's also important to keep your social media information private — your Facebook, Twitter, and Instagram — especially if you like to check in and share your location.

When you're planning your first date be sure to meet in a public place, during the day, with lots of people around. A coffee shop usually works great. Let a friend know where you'll be, who you'll be with, and when you'll be back.

Hopefully it'll be a nice date with a good guy who'll make the whole process worth it.

15.

How to Spot a Good Guy

A good, thoughtful guy will go out of his way to get to know you when you're first "meeting" online.

He'll Read Your Profile

When he contacts you, you'll be able to tell he's read your profile. He may mention something he liked about your profile. Or he might point out something you share in common. This lets you know he's actually read your profile and he's interested in getting to know you.

That will feel very different from a guy who just says, "I liked your profile." He may have read it — or not.

He'll Introduce Himself

A good guy will want to make a good first impression so he'll put some thought into what he writes. He may not be the best writer. But a genuine, heartfelt introduction can give you a nice sense of who he is.

He definitely won't copy and paste a generic message that says something like, "To learn more about me, check out my profile."

He'll Remember Who You Are

A good guy may not remember everything about you or everything you tell him. But, he'll remember your important information and the significant stuff you've shared. And if he forgets or mixes something up, he won't mind when you let him know.

If a guy can't remember your basic information, he might be pursuing too many women and that's why he can't keep his facts straight.

He Won't Just Send You a "Wink" or a "Meet Me"

If a guy "winks" at you, there's a good chance he's just seen your picture and hasn't even looked at your profile. He may not be serious about the online dating process. He may not even be looking for love.

If you want to give him the benefit of the doubt, "wink" back at him. If he still doesn't go out of his way to get to know you, he's probably not your guy.

IV.
First Date Do's and Don'ts

16.

First Date Tips to Leave Him Wanting More

A first date can be both exciting and scary. You wonder, *Will he like me? Could he be the one?* I got the best dating advice from Andrew Whaling when I attended his Pasadena Sunday Night Singles Group. Here are some tips from him, and tips from me, for a good first date.

Dealing with "Nerves"

Fear of rejection is probably the biggest hurdle to overcome on a first date. Whaling's suggestion is to shift the focus. Instead of worrying about if he will like you, remember this is your chance to get to know him and decide if *you* like him. I know this is easier said than done. But if you're smiling and meeting men and dating three people (as Whaling recommends) it does take some of the pressure off. You can relax and enjoy yourself more because each date doesn't have to lead to marriage.

Think the Opposite of "The Bachelor"

Whaling also suggests keeping your dates low-key. You want to make sure you have a chance to get to know him and to see if you enjoy each other's company. If you're in a super romantic setting or doing a high adrenaline activity it's hard to know if you're excited about the person or the activity.

Don't Bond Until You Know Him

Remember, it takes three to six months for infatuation to wear off. So, you don't want to get too bonded before then. This means not getting physical. Because the more physical you get, the more bonded you'll be. According to Brizendine, you start releasing hormones and bonding with a 20-second hug. So no slow dancing on a first date! Whaling suggests a goodnight kiss. But for a lot of women, even that makes them want to get married. So sometimes a quick hug is better.

Brizendine highlights research that suggests men bond after high-stress activities like a physical challenge. So, no hang gliding or jumping out of airplanes on a first date!

Keep the Conversation Light

I love Whaling's idea that the only goal of a first date is to decide: *Do I want a second date?* Here are Whaling's suggested topics of conversation for a first date.

- Hobbies/Interests

- Entertainment

- Leisure/Books

- Places you've been

- Sports

- Accomplishments (a little)

- Also: News, Food, a little bit about Work/Career/Profession

Don't Go There Yet

Whaling suggests staying away from topics that are too serious or personal. It doesn't mean these aren't important topics to discuss. It's just too soon. Here are Whaling's topics to avoid on a first date:

- Health problems
- Any and all complaints
- Religion/Politics/Beliefs
- Assets/Earnings/Finances
- China patterns
- Sex
- Past Relationships/Ex
- How many children you want

You Can Have Too Much of a Good Thing

It can be easy to get too intense or let the date go too long (Whaling recommends two hours max) if you really like him and are clicking. But too much too soon can be a red flag. Remember, the faster he comes on the faster he'll go away. So, if you keep your boundaries, it will weed out men who want instant closeness. The key is to leave him wanting more (not less) of you.

Is Your Conversation Flowing?

Is there a nice back and forth? You ask a question, he answers. He asks, you answer. This won't be completely even. Sometimes one person is more introverted and the other more extroverted. Or he might be nervous. But give and take is a sign of generosity, which is an important quality to look for.

Do You Want a Second Date?

After your first date, Whaling suggests reflecting and asking yourself how you felt while you were with your date. Did you feel good about yourself or not so much? What about afterward?

If you feel good about yourself and you'd like to see him again, woo-hoo! Time for a second date. But remember to keep your dates two to three weeks apart. Otherwise, you're in a relationship and you can't see anyone else. This also means keeping calls and texts to a minimum; basically just do enough to set up your next date. I know it's not very romantic. But this is how you get to know him slowly. And that's how you'll find someone you could really love and who will really love you back. And *that* is really romantic and worth waiting for.

17.

Five Questions to Avoid on a First Date

Sometimes it's hard to know how much is too much sharing on a first date. The key is to maintain your boundaries and to keep it light.

Here are some questions that you want to stay away from:

1. What Happened in Your Last Relationship?

It's normal to want to know your date's relationship history. But according to Whaling, a first date is too soon to be talking about the ex.

Relationship and addiction expert Terry Gorski also emphasizes the need to pace yourself in a new relationship so you don't get too intense too quickly. If you want someone who is the whole package, it's important to build the relationship in stages. The first stage is *Acquaintanceship/Casual Contact*. You're finding out if you enjoy hanging out together. Do you get along? Would you like to get together again? So, as hard as it sounds, try to relax and enjoy the ride.

2. How's the Dating Site Working for You?

This question is especially tricky. Sharing your online dating horror stories is a quick and easy way to bond. But, just like it's too soon to be talking about the ex, you don't want to be sharing about other people you're meeting on the dating site.

This is kind of a lose-lose situation. If your online dating experiences have been awful, you're sort of complaining and gossiping (which makes you look bad). And if you share that your online dating experiences have been great, that could make your date feel really weird. Better to just stay away from this topic altogether.

3. Why Are You Still Single?

This is my personal favorite! It sounds like a compliment — How could someone as fabulous as you still be available? But what's really being asked is, *What's wrong with you? You look okay. But I just want to cut to the chase and know why no one else wanted you so I can move on.*

4. Do You Want to Get Married?

This is a great question. And you want to find out what the other person is looking for before too long. But, a more important question is: Are you married now?

I'm not talking about someone who's cheating (though that's something to watch for). I'm talking about a date with someone who's not all the way divorced. Maybe he's separated and going through a divorce. He might even be "separated" but living in the same house with his wife, especially in today's economy. Trust me, you don't want to get in the middle of that. In fact, Whaling says it's a good idea to wait a year after a divorce is final before dating because people need time to grieve and heal. So, if he's not all the way divorced or if he hasn't had time to finish his grieving, he's not ready to start a relationship with you.

5. Do You Want Kids?

Again, a great question to ask, but definitely not on a first date. Women usually have a stronger need to have children than men do. So, if you bring this up right away, he'll think you just want him for his baby-making potential. It doesn't mean you can't find out where he stands on kids, especially if your clock is ticking. But a first date is still probably too soon.

18.

Who Pays on a First Date?

Whether it's in the line at Starbucks or when the waitress brings the check, at some point you have to decide — who pays for the first date?

The Man Usually Pays

I hate to say it because it sounds so traditional. But most of the time women expect, and men assume, that he's the one who will pay.

What if You Asked Him?

It's a nice gesture to offer to pick up the tab if you asked him out. But most women still appreciate it if the gentleman overrides them and offers to pay on the first date. I think it goes back to that "provider" feeling. It makes a woman feel taken care of.

This can be a real financial challenge to men. So, don't be disappointed if your first dates are a little low-key. Inexpensive first dates like coffee or lunch are actually better. That way you can get to know him in a low-pressure setting before either of you invests yourself more deeply —financially, or otherwise.

Avoiding the Awkward Moments

So, how do you navigate the logistics? When it comes time to pay the bill, his simple, "I've got this," says it all. And remember, this is just for the first date. If you continue to see him, it's nice for you to start pitching in at some point.

It doesn't have to be: "Let's split the bill. I had the salad. You had the chicken." It can be: "You got dinner. How about if I get the movie?" Or: "You've taken me out several times. Maybe I could bring a picnic or make you dinner next time?"

It won't be even-steven. But your gesture to contribute shows that you appreciate his generosity and that you're aware that he's not made of money.

Being a Gracious Guest

I don't know if this is still true, but traditionally, a woman wouldn't order the most expensive item on the menu. I know it's old school. But it's important to be sensitive to the fact that you are his guest. One way to do this is to order something in the middle price range.

A First and Last Date Story

I remember a first date where all I ordered was soup. And the guy still wanted to split the bill. I wasn't really having a great time anyway. But it really felt bad that he couldn't pick up this small amount. And then he tried to go in for a kiss in the parking lot. Let's just say we didn't go out again.

V.
Now You're Dating

19.

Great Dates that Won't Break the Bank

Since the guy usually pays, it's only fair to offer some inexpensive date ideas so he doesn't go broke. (You could also offer to contribute by bringing the picnic or snacks.) Here are some of my favorite low-key dates.

Coffee

Coffee makes a great first date. It's quick. It's casual. And it's pretty low stress. There are other people around, which is important in the beginning. And you still have a chance to talk and get to know him.

A Hike

Once you know him better and you feel safe with him, a hike can be really nice. You can pack a picnic or bring some snacks to share. You'll have his undivided attention. There's lots of time to talk. And there's often an opportunity for chivalry. I fell in love when my husband carried my small dog over a stream on our third date.

A Walk by the Water

If you live near a lake or the ocean, a walk by the water can be very romantic. He might even hold your hand while you walk and chat. You're out in nature. And there's usually a place to grab something to eat or drink.

Museums

Local museums can be really nice. You walk around together and "ooh" and "ahh" at the art. You get to share your interests and tastes. Sometimes, there are short films or interactive exhibits you can experience together. And there is usually an inexpensive place that has pretty good food.

Live Music – Coffee House

Some coffee houses have live music on the weekends. It can be a little noisy. But it's a relaxing way to hang out together and talk between sets in a low-key setting. The music gives you something new to talk about. And if you want to talk while the music's playing, you have to lean in close.

Concert in the Park

A lot of towns have free concerts in the park during the summer. You can bring lawn chairs or a blanket to sit on, and a picnic to share. It's a nice way to get outdoors and be with people and yet still be together. There are usually listings on the city's website with dates for the different types of music (i.e. old-ies, swing, rock, pop, jazz, etc.).

"Old Town"

Does your local town have a downtown or main street that's kind of cool? These are great places to window shop, hang out at a bookstore, and grab a cup of coffee. You get to see which book sections he likes. And you get to share your favorites. Is he a motorcycle magazine guy? You might prefer self-help or the relationship section. Maybe you both like the travel section. Then, you can share about places you've been or would like to go.

What's important is getting to know each other in a low-key setting and doing something you both enjoy. And it doesn't have to cost a lot!

20.

Five Steps to Building a Healthy Relationship

So, how do you find a healthy relationship? The best way to do this is to develop the relationship slowly, step by step.

Gorski, in his book *Getting Love Right*, has developed a practical step-by-step framework for building a relationship one stage or level at a time.

1. Can You Hang Out Together?

Gorski calls this the *Acquaintanceship* stage. This is a stage of casual contact when you're first getting to know each other. You're just sharing basic information. And you're finding out if he will treat you with common courtesy and respect.

If you tend to get intense right away, this step is extra important. In a long-term relationship, things aren't always intense. Most of your time will be spent in the day-to-day routine of life. It's important to be comfortable enjoying each other's company in a low-key way.

2. Do You Have Stuff in Common?

In Gorski's *Companionship* stage you're discovering if you have any shared hobbies or interests. You don't have to have everything in common. But it definitely helps if you have some things you like doing together.

This is also when you start to share your friends and your worlds with each other. If he doesn't introduce you to his friends or share some of his hobbies or interests with you, it might mean he doesn't have any (which is a red flag). Or, it could mean he is intentionally keeping you out of his life (an even bigger red flag — he may be hiding something).

3. Are You Friends?

In Gorski's *Friendship* stage, you begin to share on a deeper level. You share more of who you are, your feelings, and your values. And you get to see how he responds. Does he listen? Does he care? Is he respectful? You also get to see if he shares. And when he does, it's your turn to be respectful and caring.

Each new stage adds another layer of depth to your relationship. And that makes it safe to move to the next level.

4. Do You Have Passion?

Developing the relationship slowly is especially important before moving on to Gorski's next stage, *Romantic Love*. That's how you know if he is safe *before* you have sex. If you have sex in the beginning, when it's mostly infatuation, you don't really know each other. Or, as Gorski points out, you're basically having sex with a stranger, which can be exciting but also dangerous.

Plus, when you wait to have sex, your passion is based on who he really is and who you really are. So, the attraction isn't going to wear off once you really get to know him. (In fact, there can be more passion because you have more trust. And that enables you to be freer with him.)

5. Are You Ready to Build a Life Together?

Gorski's last stage is *Committed Love*. This is when you decide that you want to stay together. You enjoy being together. You have things in common. You care about each other. And you have passion. So, you commit to working things out and sticking around when things get tough. You decide to make a long-term permanent commitment to each other.

It's normal to be a little bit afraid, because love is always a risk. But, it doesn't have to be a risk taken on blind faith. Since you've built your relationship one step at a time, you really know him and he really knows you. So, your commitment is less like jumping off a cliff and more like stepping off a curb — into your new life together.

21.

Do You Need to Take it Slow?

We're drawn to people because they're different from us. They complement us. That's why two people rarely want the same amount of closeness or space all the time. This also plays out in dating. One person usually needs to take it slow. And the other person usually wants to jump right in. When you understand your different needs, you can find a pace that works for both of you. And you can both get the space and the closeness you need.

Personality Differences

When it comes to personality styles, you're often attracted to your opposite, according to authors David Keirsey and Marilyn Bates. If you're more introverted, you prefer one-on-one time together. And you need time alone to recharge your batteries. If you're more extroverted, you prefer big groups and activities with lots of people. And you need time with people to recharge your batteries.

So, an introvert might enjoy an intimate dinner for two, with lots of personal sharing, while an extrovert might enjoy a date to the fair or a concert, with lots of people around and minimal time sharing. An introvert might need more time alone, while an extrovert might get overwhelmed with too much intense one-on-one sharing. Both need space, but in different ways.

Closeness-Distance Styles

Some people build relationships very slowly and are cautious about getting too close, too fast, while others want more closeness and tend to jump into a relationship really fast, right away.

It helps to remember that you both want closeness. People who crave closeness usually didn't get enough closeness growing up. So, they're afraid they're going to lose the relationship. People who need more space often felt hurt growing up. So, they want closeness, but they just don't want to get hurt again. If you can take it slow, you can build up trust so that you can both get what you need.

Family-of-Origin Backgrounds

If you had the kind of family where everyone was in everyone else's business and there wasn't a lot of personal space, that's what love feels like to you. If your family emphasized privacy and lots of time and space for yourself, that's what love feels like to you.

As long as neither family was really extreme, there's no good or bad. In fact, people tend to gravitate toward their opposites in terms of family style.

Tips if You Need More Space:

Ask for the Space You Need
Otherwise, you'll just end up running away.

Be Specific

"I'd love to get together again. But I need to go slow. How about next week?"

Don't Feel Guilty

It's okay to go at the pace that feels right to you.

Pay Attention

If he doesn't respect your timing or your need for space, that's a red flag.

Don't Go Too Slow

And don't take too much space. Otherwise, according to attachment expert Phil Shaver, you can forget the things you like about him and lose interest altogether.

Remember, Opposites Attract

If he comes from a big noisy family, that's not a bad thing. In fact, in can be kind of fun at times.

Tips if You Need More Closeness:

Never Try to Force Closeness

Don't try to push him to go faster than he's ready for. You'll just push him further away. But if you respect his pace and timing, he'll feel safe and be able to move closer to you.

Remember, He May Need You *More*

If he needs more space, he may actually need love *more*. He's just afraid of getting hurt.

Don't Lash Out

If he's not ready to get serious or make a commitment when you are, lashing out will just confirm his fears that it's not safe to get too close to you.

Reach Out to Friends

Do an extroverted group activity to meet some of your needs for interaction with more people.

Pay Attention

If he is frequently backing up or jumping out of the relationship, that's different. That's a red flag. But, if he's slowly moving forward, that's a good sign that he can trust you more and more.

Remember, Opposites Attract

If he needs more privacy, that's not a bad thing. And you might even find you enjoy a little time and space to yourself every once in awhile.

The most important thing to remember is that you can find a way to work out your different needs for space and closeness. You can build trust with each other. And that can be very healing for both of you. If you need more space, you can learn that it's safe to get closer and that you won't get hurt. And if you need more closeness, you can learn that he may need space at times, but he's really not going anywhere.

22.

What Men Really Want (It's Not What You Think!)

Men exist in a world of competition. They compete and compare themselves with other men all the time. That's why it's so important for them to feel safe in their intimate relationships, because they don't really get that anywhere else.

Men are more independent by nature. This gets reinforced growing up, especially by their dads — think about the phrase, "Be a man" — it means refrain from showing emotion. And a man's primary way of relating to other men is through activities like work, sports, and hobbies. So, most of their conversations tend to revolve around these shared interests and activities. They rarely open up to each other for support like women do.

That's where you come in. For most men, you're it. You're all he's got.

And what he really wants is to be close to you.

So, how can you connect with him?

Find some shared activities you both enjoy. It might be watching a favorite TV show, taking a hike together, going to a ballgame or museum. And yes, his favorite shared activity will always be sex. But, there are other things he'd like to do with you too.

Remember, there are differences between how men and women think about closeness. Women think of closeness as a heart-to-heart talk with a girlfriend. But men rarely want to be this open. It feels too vulnerable to them. That's why they'd rather just figure things out for themselves.

Practice talking through important things without it turning into a fight. This is how he learns that it's safe to talk and open up to you.

Listen to him. Every now and then, if he's learned to trust you and if he's going through something particularly difficult, he may reach out to you for support. He might just want a sounding board. Or he might want suggestions and feedback. Ask him and he'll let you know what he really wants.

VI.

Dealing with Fear of Commitment

23.

Is He Ready to Commit?

We all want someone to love who really loves us. But how do you know if he is ready to take things to the next level?

Here are ten ways to know if he is ready for a real relationship:

1. Does he keep small commitments, like being on time and calling when he says he will?

2. Does he continue to move forward in your relationship? Or does he start out strong, but then have doubts or need to

take "breaks"? Remember, the faster he comes on, the faster he will go away.

3. Is he finished with his last relationship? If he's separated, recently divorced, or coming off a breakup, he's not ready to commit to a new relationship. And of course, if he's still hanging out with his ex, he's definitely not ready for anything real with you.

4. Does he ever mention wanting to "see other people"? Big red flag. He's definitely not ready to commit to a relationship.

5. If he hasn't asked you to be exclusive, assume that you're not.

6. Do you take priority on the weekends, especially Friday and Saturday nights? That means he's not out there looking for something better.

7. Has he introduced you to any of his friends or family? This doesn't happen all at once. But if he slowly begins to share his world with you, that's definitely a good sign.

8. If he is a workaholic, alcoholic, or even a sexaholic, he's not ready to commit. His obsession or addiction will always come before you.

9. If he tells you he's not ready to settle down or he's not "the marrying kind," BELIEVE HIM! He's definitely not ready for a commitment now and he may NEVER be!

10. If he keeps his small commitments to you, if you continue to grow closer, if he's making you a priority in his life and including you in his world, you're definitely headed in the right direction. And when he's ready to commit, you'll be able to trust that it's real.

24.

How to Avoid Men Who Cheat

When it comes to choosing a partner, is there anything you can do to steer clear of the cheaters?

There are no guarantees. But here are five things you can do to stack the odds in your favor:

1. Run Away from Your Type

We tend to be attracted to men who are like our parents, even if we don't want the same kind of relationship our parents had. And if there was any infidelity or divorce in your family, it can leave you feeling needy and insecure. Without realizing it, you might be attracted to men who can't commit or be faithful. And that just reinforces your insecurity. That's why it's important to consider dating guys who aren't your "type."

2. Remember — If He's Cheated Before, There's a Good Chance He'll Cheat Again

The best predictor of future behavior is past behavior. So, if he's been unfaithful in the past it may happen again under similar circumstances. And if there is *a pattern* of infidelity, there's a good chance it will happen again. So, unless he deals with the reasons he's cheated, why would you risk your heart with him? Yes, there are always exceptions, especially for the young. But, as Greg Behrendt and Liz Tuccillo remind us in *He's Just Not That Into You*, it's best to think of yourself as the rule, not the exception.

3. Go Slow and Really Get to Know Him

Remember, the first three to six months is a period of infatuation, so you don't want to get too serious before then. According to

Brizendine, it's like being on drugs in terms of your brain chemistry and hormones. And she points out that the centers in your brain that manage anxiety can get really quiet, so it's easy to miss the red flags that everyone else can see. And don't get physical right away because then you're bonded to him. And he may not be bonded to you.

4. Believe Him If He Says He's Not Ready to Settle Down

Most men aren't into commitment and marriage the same way women are. Instead, they warm up to the idea as they fall in love with you. They don't want anyone else to have you. So, they realize they better do something to get you off the market. But if he doesn't warm up to the idea of commitment and you have to rope him into it or give him an ultimatum, that's not a good sign. It could be that he's not ready for commitment or it could be that he's not ready to commit to you. Either way, actions speak louder than words. So pay attention to what his words and actions are telling you.

5. Value Yourself

We attract people who are as healthy as we are. So, the best insurance against choosing someone who might cheat or leave is to become emotionally healthy yourself. This might include counseling, or a 12-step program or other support group. Whatever works for you. What's important is that if you feel valued and valuable, you'll be able to tell when a man is treating you right and when he's not.

25.

Could You Be Afraid of Closeness?

Do you ever wonder why the men you're really into aren't that into you or why you don't like the ones who are into you?

It might be that you haven't met someone who's right for you yet. Or the guys who aren't into you have trouble with intimacy and closeness. But, if *all* the men you like aren't into you and if you *rarely* like the ones who are into you, it might mean that at some level you're afraid of closeness and commitment.

I know it sounds crazy. But that might actually be why you find those unavailable guys attractive — because they aren't into you. (Plus, they probably remind you of your father or your family.) But if that's what your father or your family were like, how would you have learned to be comfortable with closeness? You probably never had any closeness. And the closeness you did have probably wasn't that great.

Don't get me wrong. I know you want love. And I know you need love. But if you didn't get the love you needed growing up, and if you haven't had good loving relationships as an adult, then intimacy and closeness can feel unfamiliar and overwhelming. You might feel vulnerable and afraid without even realizing it.

So, what can you do? Sometimes it helps to think about:

- How would it feel if you had the kind of love and closeness you really want?

- What about that kind of love and closeness might feel scary? (Do you have any fears of rejection or getting hurt?)

- How could you get close and risk in little ways to see if the other person is safe before you get closer and risk more?

- Would you ever want to share your vulnerable feelings and fears with him? (How he responds will tell you if it's safe to share more.)

When you only date men who aren't really available, you play it safe. You might get hurt. But you've been there before and you know what that's like. It's a bigger risk to actually get close to someone who won't run away. Because then you're in uncertain waters. But, if you go slow, you can test the waters to see if you want to go any further. You don't have to jump in the deep end. In fact, it's probably better not to. Instead, you can start in the shallow end and just move forward one little step at a time.

26.

Quiz — Are You Ready for Love?

Does it ever feel like all the good ones are already taken? And the guys you meet just aren't relationship material? Or when you meet someone you do like, he's just not that into you?

A lot of good men are already married. But there are plenty of other great guys still out there. But if you can't seem to find one, it might mean at some level that *you're not quite ready for love.*

It's hard to believe, I know. Everyone around you is pairing up and settling down.

And you don't want to be left behind. But there may be a part of you that is holding back.

Take this simple quiz to find out.*

Are You Sure You're Ready for Love?
(Choose as many as apply)

Do you have relationships with men who:

    a. want to marry you after 6 to 16 months? (0 points)

    b. want to marry you at first, but then get cold feet? (1 point)

    c. don't know if they ever want to get married? (1 point)

When a guy you like wants to get closer:

    a. do you say, "Come here, Baby!" (0 points)

    b. does he become less attractive? (1 point)

    c. do you get nervous? (1 point)

When you think about sharing your life with someone, do you:

    a. feel elated! (0 points)

    b. secretly wonder if you'll have to give

up important parts of your single life?
(1 point)

c. worry you might lose yourself?
(1 point)

If you scored 1 to 3 points, you may have mixed feelings about finding love. If you scored 4 to 6 points, you may have a fear of finding love. If you scored 0 points you could be ready for love!

Take Action:

If you have mixed feelings or if you have a fear of finding love, this is not a life sentence. It just means at some level, you may have a fear of intimacy. Part of you really wants love. But another part of you is afraid you won't get what you really need in a relationship.

Sometimes it means you're afraid of getting hurt. Sometimes it means you're afraid of getting close and then losing him. Sometimes it's a little of both. And now that you know you're not quite ready for love, you can do something about it.

* This quiz is not a valid psychological assessment tool.

VII.

Surviving Holidays and Special Occasions

27.

A Valentine's Day Antidote — Girls Night IN!

A Girls Night Out can help you get through Valentine's Day if you're single.

But, there's always the chance that having dinner next to all those happy couples will make you feel worse. And if you opt for a bar instead of a restaurant, there's an even greater chance you'll drink too much and end up with someone you wouldn't normally choose.

So, what's a girl to do?

Have A Girls Night IN!

Get your single girlfriends together. Have everyone bring something to eat or drink. Make sure whoever is hosting the get together has Netflix or Hulu or something good you can watch. You might choose something romantic or a good breakup movie, like *500 Days of Summer*. This can be whatever you want!

This is your night to be with good friends who love and support you. You can keep the conversation light. Or you can share from the heart. You can:

- Yell or cry or laugh about not being in a relationship

- Talk about why you're glad you're single today

- Talk about what you wish your Valentine's Day was like

- Talk about what you want in a man or in a relationship

- Talk about what you'll do to make changes in yourself or your relationships this year

- Not talk about men or relationships at all

- Enjoy a good movie, good friends, good food, and good drinks

Whatever you do, remember how awesome you are. And that Valentine's Day is just one day. Everything will look and feel better tomorrow.

28.

How to Cure a Valentine's Day Hangover

Valentine's Day can be hard if you're single. All those hearts and flowers and cards can leave you with a Valentine's Day hangover.

So, what's the best remedy?

Count Your Blessings

I know it's hard to be single, especially on Valentine's Day. But it's important to remember that being in a bad relationship is way worse than being alone.

Appreciate Your Gal Pals!

Do you have a best friend or several good girlfriends who are single? Now that all the Valentine's hoopla has died down, get your-selves together for a spa day, a shopping day, or a fancy dinner out. It doesn't matter what you do as long as it's fun and maybe even a little extravagant!

Me Time

What is a favorite treat for you? It could be painting pots or sitting down with a great novel and a cup of coffee. Whatever makes you feel happy and good, just do it! And enjoy some quality time with yourself.

Take Two Baby Steps and Call Me in the Morning

What are two things you could do toward finding your Mr. Right? Is there a class or event you could attend that attracts good guys? Has a friend offered to fix you up with someone she thinks is really special? Could you start smiling and making eye contact the next time some-one nice looks your way? You'd be surprised what happens when you let the universe know you're ready to meet someone good.

Remember, You're a Catch!

You deserve a special guy who appreciates just how special you are. Don't settle for anything less!

29.

A Single Girl's Summer Survival Guide

When summer comes around things can get tricky — especially if you're single.

- Where will you go on vacation this year? Who will you go with?

- Are there any weddings to attend? Should you bring a date or go alone?

- What about baby showers?

- Maybe a summer fling would make you feel better?

Here are a few suggestions to help you survive this season.

Weddings are Not Mandatory

You love your friend and you're genuinely happy for her. But it's hard to keep going to weddings single. So, let me start by saying you don't HAVE to go. If the best you can do is send a gift and wish the couple well, that's okay. Everyone likes something from their gift registry. Order online unless you want to visit the wedding section at your local department store.

Should You Bring a Date to a Wedding?

If you'd like to go to the wedding, should you bring a date or go solo? Weddings are an intense date unless you're in a committed relationship. It makes men feel really pressured. So, it might be better to bring a friend. Or you can even go alone if you're feeling brave. Besides, there may be some interesting guys at the wedding. Just beware of guys looking to hook up with single girls who've had too much champagne.

What About Baby Showers?

Your friends have graduated from weddings to babies. Again, if you're just not up to going, that's okay. *Goodnight Moon* and *Pat the Bunny* are great baby books. And you can get them both online.

Where to Go for Your Vacation

You deserve a vacation just like all the couples and families you know. You can go alone or ask a close friend. If you're going solo, choose some place extra safe. I'm in SoCal and I like Santa Barbara. It's just a couple hours drive from Los Angeles. There's the pier and lots of fun things to do and see. Ask around for local vacation spots near you. And stay away from known couples locations. (Cambria is a romantic spot on the California Central Coast. But, if you're single, all that handholding can be depressing.)

What to Do on Your Vacation

If you like crowds, check out the local tourist attractions. If you want privacy, find a quiet place to read or walk. When it comes to eating out, dinner is the trickiest. A fancy restaurant may not be best. But a neighborhood eatery can be friendly and inviting. And avoid going to bars alone. If you're feeling lonely, it can be a recipe for disaster.

A Summer Fling Can Be Inviting

When you're feeling discouraged, it's easy to go for Mr. Right Now instead of waiting for Mr. Right. And if it happens, don't beat yourself up. But remember, every detour takes you off the path of finding what you really want — a good man by *your* side at *your* wedding, who wants to make babies and spend the rest of his vacations with *you*. And that is worth waiting for.

30.

Who Will You Be Kissing Under the Mistletoe?

The holidays can be challenging if you're single. But it's also a great time to meet someone new!

You're out and about more. You're seeing people you haven't seen in a while.... So, how do you maximize those holiday opportunities?

Just Say "YES!"

Whether it's a work party, a family party, a friend's party... when those holiday invites start rolling in, just say "yes"! You never know where you might meet someone really interesting. And when it's time for the party, get yourself up and out the door!

Host Your Own Holiday Get Together

Have your own party and invite your single friends. Tell each of them to bring their single friends. This is a great way to meet quality singles because you and your friends have already pre-screened everyone!

Practice Flirting

Remember to smile and make eye contact. even if it's just for a second. That's how you let a good guy know you're open to being approached.

Run Away from Your "Type"

Remember, if a relationship with your type hasn't worked in the past, there's a good chance it won't work in the future. According to Lewis, Amini & Lannon, that kind of initial chemistry just means he's a perfect fit for all that hardwiring in your brain from your family-of-origin. So, if you don't want a repeat of your past relationships, or you don't want the kind of relationships you saw growing up, initial chemistry may not be your friend. (You can still have chemistry, it just may take a few dates to kick in.)

Turn the Tables

It's inevitable. There are some people that you only see during the holidays. And somehow, they can never resist asking, "So, are you seeing anyone?" This is your opportunity to put them to work. Let them know that you're not currently with anyone. But if they know of someone good, you'd be open to being set up. (This works great, as long as your potential "matchmaker" has a good relationship of their own. You don't want someone who is a "bad picker" picking someone for you!)

31.

My Holiday Wish for You – Let Love Find You

As the holidays draw near and you look ahead to another year, you may be wondering, *When will I ever find someone to love me?*

There are lots of things you can do and places you can go to meet men. But sometimes it's as simple as allowing love to find you. In other words, don't block love from coming to you.

I know that sounds crazy. I know you want to find someone more than anything. I know you hate being single, especially during the holidays.

But, what if you didn't have to *do* anything to find love?

What if you just had to let down the wall? What if you just need to open yourself up? What if the man who could really love you and treat you right is waiting for you — and all you have to do is let him in?

I know what you're saying.

Part of you is saying, *Hell, yea!*

But the other part of you, the *Oh-my-god-what-if-I-get-hurt* part of you is saying *HOLD ON*. The *What-if-he-doesn't-like-me-once-he-gets-to-know-me* part of you is saying, *Let's not get carried away here!* The *I-don't-feel-good-enough-about-myself* part of you is saying, *What's the rush?*

And that's what may be keeping you from finding love.

So, tell that scared part of you...

Yes, it's important to heal the hurts that have drawn you to the wrong guys in the past. And yes, it's important to go slow so you can spot red flags and screen out the players.

But if you want to find a good guy, there comes a time when you have to take a deep breath and take a risk. Not a big jumping-off-a-cliff kind of risk. Just a stepping-off-a-curb baby step kind of risk.

You put yourself out there and you allow someone to get close to you.

When you meet someone nice and good and fun, you let him in. Bit by bit, you let down the wall. You open yourself up. And you let him love you — the way you deserve to be loved.

That's my wish for you — that you let love find you. Because it really is out there. Your guy is waiting for you. It's okay to let him in.

And I do wish you a New Year full of love!

references

Behrendt, G. & Tuccillo, L. (2004). *He's Just Not That Into You*. New York: Simon & Schuster.

Brizendine, L. (2006). *The Female Brain*. New York: Doubleday.

Gorski, T. (1993). *Getting Love Right: Learning the choices of healthy intimacy*. New York: Simon & Schuster.

Keirsey, D. & Bates, M. (1984). *Please Understand Me: Character & temperament types*. Del Mar, California: Prometheus.

Lewis, T., Amini, F., & Lannon, R. (2000). *A General Theory of Love*. New York: Random.

Shaver, Phil. (2008, November). Romantic Love, Caregiving and Sex: Implications of attachment research for couple therapy. *Keeping Love Alive: Desire, monogamy and the neurobiology of intimate attachments.* The Fourth Anatomy of Intimacy Conference. Sponsored by the Department of Psychiatry and Human Behavior, UCI, and the Foundation for the Contemporary Family in collaboration with the Lifespan Learning Institute. UC Irvine.

Whaling, A. (2000-2002). *Sunday Night Singles*. Pasadena, CA.

about the author

Dr. Vonda ("Vondie") Lozano is a California Licensed Marriage and Family Therapist and Certified Hypnotherapist. She was previously on faculty at Azusa Pacific University and University of La Verne. She has been featured in *Cosmopolitan*, the *Wall Street Journal*, and on KABC Talk Radio. Vondie is the author of two ebooks, *How to Let Go of the Past* and *Date, Don't Mate*. She lives in Ventura with her husband and their dog.

www.vondielozano.com